THE 1976 BUDGET

Short-Run Stabilization Policy and the Long-Run Budget Outlook

David J. Ott and Attiat F. Ott

American Enterprise Institute for Public Policy Research
Washington, D. C.

This is the fifth study to result from AEI's Long Range Budget Projection Project. Contributors to this volume are the late DAVID J. OTT, professor of economics at Clark University and director of the project, and ATTIAT F. OTT, also professor of economics at Clark University.

The authors wish to thank William Fellner for his helpful comments and suggestions. In addition, thanks are due Professor Lawrence J. Korb of the U.S. Coast Guard Academy for projecting the defense budget, Armando Baquiero for projecting commerce and transportation, health, manpower, and other areas, and James J. Breen for projecting OASDI, as well as for refining and running the 1975 AEI-BRAP Model. However, only the authors are responsible for the findings of this study or for any errors that might remain.

ISBN 0-8447-3168-4

Domestic Affairs Study 32, June 1975

Library of Congress Catalog Card No. 75-18627

Printed in the United States of America

To the memory of
David J. Ott

CONTENTS

THE 1976 BUDGET

1. Introduction

In February 1974 the President's Council of Economic Advisers (CEA) mirrored the consensus among economic forecasters when it concluded that "1974 would be a year of little output growth and considerable inflation but that in both respects the second half of the year should be much better than the first." [1] The CEA's view was that the adjustment to spending more money on imported oil would be completed early in the year and that, subsequently, expansionary forces, particularly rising expenditures on housing and automobiles, would lead to a revival in the second half of the year.[2] The fiscal year 1975 budget was seen as appropriate to this scenario. On the assumption that real gross national product (GNP) would rise only slightly in 1974 and that prices (as measured by the GNP deflator) would rise by about 7 percent, the budget would be essentially neutral: that is, the full-employment surplus would remain essentially unchanged from its level of $6 billion in 1974. This budget posture, combined with growth in the broadly defined money stock (M_2) of 8 percent in 1974, was viewed as consistent with the CEA forecast.

However, by the time final decisions had to be made on the fiscal year 1976 budget program, the outlook had changed markedly. Real output, after declining through the first half of the year, did not make the expected recovery. Instead, beginning in October 1974, the economy slipped into its steepest decline since 1937, with real GNP in the fourth quarter of 1974 almost 5 percent lower than a year

[1] *Report of the Council of Economic Advisers* (Washington, D. C.: Government Printing Office, 1974), p. 43.

[2] Ibid., p. 29.

Table 1

FULL-EMPLOYMENT SURPLUS OR DEFICIT, 1973–74[a]

($ in billions)

Year	Quarter	Federal	State and Local	Total
1973	I	−5.1	14.7	9.6
	II	−0.1	12.3	12.2
	III	7.7	11.2	18.9
	IV	8.6	8.1	16.7
1974	I	16.6	10.9	27.5
	II	22.9	12.6	35.5
	III	30.4	15.4	45.8
	IV	22.8	19.1	42.3
1973[b]		2.7	11.6	14.4
1974[b]		23.2	14.5	37.7

[a] Quarterly data, seasonally adjusted at annual rates, NIA basis.

[b] Calendar year.

Source: 1973-I through 1974-III, from *Annual Report of the Council of Economic Advisers*, 1975, p. 64; 1974-IV, authors' estimates.

earlier. Meanwhile, the rate of inflation in 1974—10.3 percent—not only turned out to be much higher than anticipated, but continued to rise through the fourth quarter of 1974, when it reached an annual rate of 13.6 percent.

Both monetary and fiscal policy turned out to be more restrictive than the CEA had earlier termed "appropriate." The full-employment surplus in the federal budget did not remain "essentially unchanged." The surplus in the federal sector of the national income accounts (NIA) rose from $8.6 billion in the fourth quarter of 1973 to about $30 billion in the third quarter of 1974 (Table 1), and the increase for the entire year 1974 over 1973 was $20.5 billion. While much of the increase in the full-employment surplus was the result, not of discretionary fiscal action, but of inflation at a higher rate than was anticipated early in the year, there was a tighter budget situation than had been expected, even after allowing for the extra inflation. Even if inflation in 1974 had proceeded at the anticipated 7 percent rate, the full-employment surplus still would have been some $11 billion higher than in 1973.

In addition, the state and local sector's full-employment surplus also became much more restrictive. From the fourth quarter of 1973 to the fourth quarter of 1974, the state and local sector's full-employment surplus rose by $11 billion (see Table 1). Thus, the *combined* full-employment surplus of the government sector rose from $14.4 billion in 1973 to $37.7 billion in 1974.

Monetary policy was also more restrictive than the CEA had hoped it would be. M_2 grew at an annual rate of 7.4 percent from December 1973 to December 1974. (M_1 grew at a 4.7 percent rate.) Moreover, since the rate of inflation was much higher than had been forecast, *real* M_2 (and M_1) declined. Monetary policy was thus even more restrictive, relative to actual economic conditions, than the slower-than-anticipated rates of growth of the monetary aggregates would suggest. And perhaps most important of all, the rates of growth of M_2 and M_1 slowed markedly in the second half of 1974, at the very time when the recession was deepening. M_2 grew at a 5.8 percent annual rate from June through December, while M_1 grew at a 3.1 percent annual rate.[3]

Thus a major concern in framing the fiscal year 1976 budget was to provide stimulus to the sagging economy. A second concern was to put together a program to achieve the administration's professed goal of reducing oil imports by 1 million barrels a day in 1975 and 2 million barrels a day in 1976.

This study first summarizes, evaluates, and compares the original budget program of the Ford administration and the budget program that resulted from actions by Congress and the administration on taxes and spending taken through the end of March, in terms of the stimulus they would provide to the economy. Then the study considers the long-run balance between federal expenditures and receipts under these alternative budget programs.

No attempt is made to assess the merits of the alternative energy programs in terms of the objective of reducing imports. However, in the following section, the energy proposals are discussed in terms of their stimulatory role.

2. Providing Fiscal Stimulus in 1975–76

In this section we will discuss the amount and the timing of the stimulus that alternative fiscal programs would provide to the economy in 1975 and 1976.

The Administration's Proposals. In his budget message to Congress, President Ford proposed a comprehensive tax/energy program de-

[3] All rates of growth of M_2 and M_1 are from the Federal Reserve Bank of St. Louis, *Monetary Trends*, March 20, 1975.

Table 2

FEDERAL GOVERNMENT RECEIPTS AND EXPENDITURES, ADMINISTRATION'S BUDGET, FISCAL YEARS 1974–76

($ in billions)

Item	1974, Actual	1975 (est.)	1976 (est.)
Unified budget basis			
Receipts	264.9	278.8	297.5
Outlays	268.4	313.4	349.4
Surplus or deficit (−)	−3.5	−34.7	−51.9
Full-employment surplus	15.0	17.0	12.0
NIA basis			
Receipts	273.6	287.6	305.1
Expenditures	278.3	323.7	361.0
Surplus or deficit	−4.7	−36.1	−55.9
Full-employment surplus[a]	11.8	17.7	13.7

[a] The NIA-basis full-employment surplus is preliminary.

Source: *The Budget of the United States Government, Fiscal Year 1976* (Washington, D.C.: U.S. Government Printing Office, 1975) and U.S. Department of Commerce, Bureau of Economic Analysis.

signed to (1) provide stimulus to the economy in 1975 and (2) reduce U.S. dependence on foreign sources of oil. Table 2 shows the overall dimensions of the administration's budget program—both on a unified budget basis and on the national income accounts (NIA) basis—and Table 3 summarizes the major features of the fiscal/energy program.

On both the unified and the NIA budget basis, budget outlays were estimated to rise sharply in fiscal 1976—by about $36 billion, or 11.5 percent. Actual receipts were estimated to rise by much less because of the sagging economy—by $18.7 billion in the unified budget (6.7 percent) and $17.5 billion (6.1 percent) in the NIA budget. The combination of rapid expenditure growth and slower growth in receipts produced unified budget deficits, estimated to be about $35 billion in fiscal 1975 and $52 billion in fiscal 1976 ($36 billion and $56 billion, respectively, on an NIA basis). However, adjusting for the shortfall in receipts and the increase in expenditures (unemployment compensation and public works employment) caused by the slack in the economy changes the original deficit calculation drastically. With the unemployment rate assumed to be 4 percent, the unified budget under the original estimates would show surpluses of

$17 billion in fiscal year 1975 and $12 billion in fiscal 1976 (about $18 billion and $14 billion, respectively, on an NIA basis).

The stimulus recommended in the budget was partly in the form of a one-time "negative surtax" or rebate of 12 percent of 1974 individual income tax liabilities (up to a maximum of $1,000) to be paid in equal installments in May and September of 1975. This would have reduced personal taxes by $12.2 million in 1975 (see Table 3). Business tax relief was recommended in the form of an increase in the investment tax credit from 7 percent (4 percent for utilities) to 12 percent on eligible machinery that was either "placed in service" in 1975 or ordered in 1975 and placed in service by the end of 1976. This would have reduced corporate taxes by $3.2 billion in 1975 and $0.8 billion in 1976 (see Table 3).

Table 3

NET FISCAL STIMULUS FROM THE ADMINISTRATION'S TAX/ENERGY PROGRAM, CALENDAR YEARS 1975–76[a]

(current $ in billions)

Item	1975	1976
(1) Fiscal stimulus	−15.6	−1.1
Personal tax rebate and personal income tax credit	(−12.4)	(−0.3)
Corporate income tax credit	(−3.2)	(−0.8)
(2) Energy taxes	26.4	30.0
(3) Energy tax offsets	−30.1	−34.0
Personal tax cuts	(−19.1)	(−19.0)
Corporate tax rate reduction	(−6.0)	(−8.0)
Special payments to nontaxpayers	(−2.0)	(−2.0)
Energy equalization grants to state/local government	(−1.5)	(−2.0)
Federal equalization purchases	(−1.5)	(−3.0)
(4) Net stimulus:		
Change in full-employment surplus [(1)+(2)+(3)]	−19.3	−5.1
(5) Actual deficit	−62.1	−39.3

[a] Effect on the full-employment surplus, NIA basis.

Source: U.S. Department of Commerce, Bureau of Economic Analysis (BEA). The $80 "negative tax" was priced out here as equivalent to an $8 billion (annual rate) permanent transfer in the third quarter of each year. BEA treats it as a $2 billion (annual rate) transfer, spread evenly over all four quarters (but effective only for the third and fourth quarters in 1975).

The reduction in oil imports was to be achieved mainly by taxes that would take about $26.4 billion out of the economy in 1975: (1) a tariff on imported oil of $2 a barrel and an excise tax of $2 a barrel and 37 cents per thousand cubic feet on natural gas ($12.3 billion), (2) price decontrol for crude oil and price deregulation for "new" natural gas, and (3) a "windfall profits" tax on crude oil ($12.1 billion).[4] The impact of these measures would be to raise oil prices and eventually other prices as well. To offset this drag on the economy, a $30.1 billion package of tax relief and expenditure increases—"energy rebates"—was proposed, including:

(1) A permanent doubling of the minimum standard deduction (low-income allowance) from $1,300 to $2,600 for a couple filing a joint return and a permanent cut in the tax rates applied to the first four income brackets, from a range of 14 to 17 percent to a range of 5 to 16 percent. These would have reduced taxes by some $19.1 billion in 1975.

(2) A permanent cut in corporate income tax rates of 6 percentage points—from 48 to 42 percent. (This would have meant a reduction of $6 billion in 1975.)

(3) An $80 payment to persons paying no taxes, as well as to certain low-income taxpayers. (The total would have been $2.0 billion in 1975.)

(4) A special energy equalization grant to state and local governments—$1.5 billion in 1975, rising to $2 billion in 1976.

(5) An allowance for the increase in federal spending due to increased energy costs in 1975—$1.5 billion, rising to $3 billion in 1976.

Table 3 summarizes the calendar year impact of the President's tax/energy program.

Since proposing the package, the President has postponed the effective date of the second stage of the tariff increase from March 1 to May 1, 1975, and the date for deregulation of the price of "old" oil has also been postponed to May 1. These actions will reduce energy taxes by about $2.3 billion in 1975 if the program is enacted with the other provisions intact.

---

[4] Other energy measures, which were recommended but which did not have major budget significance, included the creation of a strategic oil reserve, expanded production from naval petroleum reserves, and protection of the domestic energy industry against "excessive risks" of abrupt declines in the price of imported oil.

Changes in the Fiscal Program. Since the administration's fiscal program was announced, major changes have occurred on both the expenditures and the receipts sides of the budget.

The administration's budget was worked up under the assumption that federal government expenditures would be held down by proposed cuts of $3.3 billion in fiscal 1975 and $17 billion in fiscal 1976. These are shown in Table 4. The proposed cuts were of two types: (1) deferrals and recisions[5] of outlays, which account for all of the $3.3 billion in cuts in fiscal 1976, and (2) the "5 percent ceiling reduction," amounts it was assumed would be saved by restraining expenditures that are tied to the cost of living, for example, federal employees' pay, social security benefits, and supplemental security income (SSI) benefits. The "5-percent ceiling" cuts account for $6 billion of the $17 billion of cuts proposed by the administration for fiscal 1976.

As of this writing, the Congress has made it clear that it will not accept the "5 percent ceiling reduction," and virtually all of the recisions have been rejected by the Congress. On a *calendar* year basis, then, another $9.3 billion of stimulus has been added in 1975 and another $15.1 billion in 1976.

The original outlay estimates have also been increased by the administration's decision, after an adverse court ruling, to release funds impounded for water, sewer, and highway grants. Although impounded funds totaled about $11 billion, the release does not mean outlays will immediately rise by anything like this amount. The effect on outlays would be about $0.5 billion in calendar 1975 and $1.5 billion in calendar 1976. In addition, the legal delay in leasing oil rights to the Atlantic offshore fields could lower federal receipts by perhaps $0.5 billion in calendar 1975 and $1.5 billion in calendar 1976.

Finally, President Ford himself has requested an additional $2 billion in funds for public employment programs in fiscal 1976. At this writing, it seems probable not only that the Congress will approve this request, but that it may even increase further the funding for these programs.

---

[5] "Deferrals" and "recisions" are terms that describe methods the President may use to reduce spending below the amount initially provided for by the Congress. A *deferral* is executive action or inaction that delays the obligation or expenditure of budget authority already provided by the Congress. A recision is congressional cancellation of previously granted budget authority. The President may institute a deferral on his own initiative, but it cannot extend beyond the end of the fiscal year and may be overturned at any time by either house of Congress. Recisions proposed by the President must be approved by both houses of Congress within forty-five days in order to become effective.

Table 4
PROGRAM CUTS PROPOSED IN THE ADMINISTRATION'S BUDGET (CHANGE IN EXPENDITURES), FISCAL YEARS 1975–76[a]
($ in billions)

Type of Expenditure and Program	1975	1976
Purchases of goods and services	−0.6	−3.7
Defense	−0.4	−2.5
5 percent ceiling	—	−1.2
Other	−0.4	−1.3
Nondefense	−0.2	−1.2
5 percent ceiling	—	−0.4
Other	−0.2	−0.8
Transfer payments to persons	−1.1	−8.4
5 percent ceiling	—	−4.4
Old age, survivors and disability insurance	—	−2.6
Federal retirement and disability	—	−0.8
Railroad retirement	—	−0.1
Supplemental Security Income	—	−0.1
Child nutrition	—	−0.1
Other	—	−0.7
Other	−1.1	−4.0
Old age, survivors, disability, and health insurance	−0.1	−0.7
Supplemental medical insurance	−0.2	−0.4
Other	−0.5	−1.2
Food stamps	−0.3	−0.7
Grants-in-aid to state and local governments	−1.3	−4.9
Public assistance grants	−0.1	−0.5
Social service grants	—	−0.5
Medicaid grants	−0.2	−0.6
Highways	−0.4	−1.6
Other (mostly EPA grants)	−0.6	−1.7
Totals		
Purchases of goods and services	−0.6	−3.7
Transfer payments to persons	−1.1	−8.4
Grants-in-aid to state and local governments	−1.3	−4.9
Total expenditure changes	−3.3[b]	−17.0
Addendum: 5 percent ceiling portion	0	−6.0

[a] NIA basis.
[b] Includes 0.3 of "exclusions."
Source: U.S. Department of Commerce, Bureau of Economic Analysis, and authors' estimates.

Table 5

POSSIBLE INCREASES IN FEDERAL EXPENDITURES OVER ADMINISTRATION'S BUDGET ESTIMATES, 1975–76[a]

(current $ in billions)

Item	1975	1976
Congressional rejection of 5 percent ceiling	2.8	3.1
Congressional rejection of other proposed spending cuts	6.4	12.0
Release of impounded funds	0.5	1.5
Delay in leasing offshore oil fields	0.5	1.5
Additional public employment funds	1.0	1.0
Total possible expenditure increase over budget estimates	11.2	19.1

[a] NIA basis.

Source: U.S. Department of Commerce, Bureau of Economic Analysis, and authors' estimates.

Table 5 summarizes these possible "add-ons" to federal spending for calendar years 1975 and 1976. Federal expenditures could be as much as $11 billion more than the budget estimates for calendar 1975. In calendar 1976, more than $19 billion of additional stimulus could come from the expenditure side of the budget.

Changes in the Tax Program. The Congress moved fairly rapidly to implement a tax program of its own design. Late in March it passed its own tax bill—the Revenue Acts of 1975 (hereinafter referred to as the congressional tax bill or the congressional tax program)—to provide fiscal stimulus, and as of this writing, the Congress is considering alternatives to the President's tax-rebate/energy program, centering on increases in excise taxes on gasoline. In this section, we will concentrate on the effect of the tax bill put together by the Congress, since the Democrats have indicated that, whatever their energy proposals, they will be a "wash" in terms of budget impact. (That is, any taxes they impose that are not rebated back to the private sector will be used for increased energy expenditure.)

Table 6 summarizes the tax package passed by the Congress, which provides about $22.5 billion of net stimulus in calendar 1975 and $5.7 billion in 1976. (The latter will rise to about $14 billion if the structural changes are made permanent.)

Table 6

NET FISCAL STIMULUS FROM THE CONGRESSIONAL TAX PROGRAM, 1975–76[a]

(current $ in billions)

Item	1975	1976
Individual	−19.7	−3.1
Individual rebate on 1974 taxes	−8.1	0
Earned income credit[b]	0	−1.5
Social security bonus	−1.7	0
Housing credit	−0.6	0
Minimum standard and standard deduction[b]	−3.7	−1.5
Exemption credit	−5.3	0
Child care deduction	−0.1	−0.1
Liberalized unemployment compensation	−0.2	0
Business	−2.8	−2.6
Change in normal corporate tax rate and base	−1.5	−1.5
Liberalized and increased investment tax credit	−3.3	−3.3
Reduced depletion allowance	+1.6	+1.6
Increase in taxation of foreign-source income	+0.4	+0.4
Net stimulus	−22.5	−5.7

[a] Effect on the full-employment surplus, NIA basis.

[b] These structural changes were put in the act for 1975 only. (The earned-income credit appears in 1976 because it is paid out after filing.) If the provisions were made permanent, the net stimulus in 1976 would be $−14.0 billion instead of $−5.7 billion.

Source: U.S. Treasury Department and estimates by authors.

The aggregate stimulus provided for 1975 is thus about $3.3 billion more than in the Ford program, although the thrust of the tax program is quite different in several respects:

(1) For individuals, much more weight is given to reductions applying to 1975 taxes than in the administration program. "One-shot" tax rebates against 1974 liabilities account for only $8.1 billion of the cuts. The other $11.6 billion of individual relief is accounted for by $9.1 billion of reductions in amounts withheld in 1975 (beginning on May 1) to reflect increased minimum standard deductions, an increase in the percentage standard deduction, the new $30 credit per exemption, and the liberalized child care deduction, along with $2.5 billion for the social security bonus, the housing credit, and extension of unem-

ployment benefits. Furthermore, the rebates are targeted more toward lower-income groups, with a maximum rebate of $200 per return.

(2) The net relief for business is smaller than in the administration proposal ($2.8 as opposed to $3.6 billion), largely because of $1.7 billion of increased taxes on oil companies losing the depletion allowance. The increase in the investment tax credit is cut back from 12 percent under the administration proposal to 10 percent, but corporate relief is provided by raising the amount of a corporation's profit to which the lower, "normal," rate of 22 percent applies from $25,000 to $50,000 and cutting the rate to 20 percent on the first $25,000. This benefits mainly small corporations.

(3) A novel new proposal is included in the bill: a 10 percent credit against earned income up to $4,000 (phasing out at $8,000) to taxpayers with children. This provides no stimulus in 1975, but results in refunds in 1976 of about $1.5 billion.

Net Fiscal Stimulus after the Expenditure and Tax Changes. The increase in expenditures over budget estimates discussed in the previous section, together with a tax cut larger than President Ford recommended, add considerably to the net stimulus from the budget in 1975 and 1976 (see Table 7). The net additional stimulus would

Table 7

NET FISCAL STIMULUS AFTER EXPENDITURE INCREASES AND CONGRESSIONAL TAX BILL INSTEAD OF ADMINISTRATION PROPOSAL, CALENDAR YEARS 1975–76[a]

(current $ in billions)

Item	1975	1976
(1) Failure to pass administration's energy/tax proposal	+19.3	+5.1
(2) Increases in expenditures (from Table 5)	−11.2	−19.1
(3) Congressional version of tax cut (Table 6)	−22.5	−5.7
(4) Additional net fiscal stimulus [(1) + (2) + (3)]	−14.4	−19.7
(5) Total net stimulus [(2) + (3)]	−33.7	−30.1
(6) Actual deficit (assuming no revenue feedback from stimulus)	−76.5	−59.0

[a] Effect on the full-employment surplus, NIA basis.

Source: U.S. Treasury Department and authors' estimates.

be $14.4 billion in 1975 and $20 billion in 1976. If the structural features of the tax bill are made permanent, then total stimulus from the budget will be about $25 billion higher in calendar 1976 than under the original budget estimates.

Effect on the Budget Deficit. If we ignore the effect that the additional fiscal stimulus might have on the gross national product forecast—the forecast on which the original estimates of revenues and the actual budget deficit were based—then the changes in expenditures and receipts discussed above would raise the deficit (on an NIA basis) from $62.1 billion to $76.5 billion in calendar 1975 and from $39.3 billion to $59 billion in calendar 1976. Over the two years the federal sector deficit would be some $135 billion. Great concern has been expressed about back-to-back deficits of this size. This issue is discussed in the following section.

3. An Evaluation of Administration and Congressional Proposals

How do the administration and congressional alternatives compare in terms of providing stimulus to the economy? To answer this question, four issues must be dealt with. The first and most basic issue is whether or not tax cuts or expenditure increases that are not accompanied by monetary expansion provide any stimulus to the economy. Second, since the largest part of the 1975 stimulus comes from tax cuts, it is important to analyze the 1975 cuts. Third, given knowledge of the stimulus that a dollar of tax relief or expenditure increase can provide, the *timing* of the stimulus is important. Finally, we must not forget the state-local sector; the overall stimulus from the government sector as a whole will depend on their balances in 1975 and 1976. In this section, each of these issues is addressed briefly.

How Stimulatory Are Tax Cuts and Expenditure Increases? Economists differ on the question whether or not tax cuts and expenditure increases will stimulate the economy. Theoretical and empirical debate on this issue has been going on over the past two decades, and while recently the theoretical discussion has succeeded in reducing to a very few the number of empirical questions that must be answered, no clearcut conclusions have been reached.

Basically the issue is simple. No one argues that a tax cut or expenditure increase does not *initially* stimulate total demand and therefore output. But cutting taxes or increasing expenditures increases the *actual* deficit in the federal budget. This in turn means that, without monetary expansion through purchases by the Federal Reserve of the new debt issued by the Treasury, the private sector must be induced to accumulate the new debt. As this occurs, the wealth of the private sector increases.[6]

The accumulated wealth in the form of government debt in the hands of the private sector produces two effects. On the one hand, an increase in the wealth of the public increases consumption expenditures and thus adds to the initial stimulative effect of the budget action. However, on the other hand, the increase in wealth increases the demand for money. Wealth-holders want to hold more cash to diversify their now larger portfolios. Without an increase in the stock of money, this causes interest rates to rise, which in turn tends to reduce nonfederal expenditures, particularly business fixed investment, housing construction expenditures, and state and local spending. The net of these two effects of the deficit—*increased* consumption vis-à-vis interest-rate-induced *decreases* in other expenditures (and perhaps consumption too)—determines whether or not the tax cut or the increase in federal expenditures will be stimulatory and, if so, how stimulatory.[7] The second effect—higher interest rates that "crowd out" private borrowing and expenditures—are a basis for the concern—so often expressed by Treasury Secretary Simon—over the size of federal deficits.

The net outcome also depends upon how the private sector views the deficit-financed government spending. If, for example, the government expenditures financed by large deficits are viewed by investors as substitutes for their own private investment, no "crowding" will take place. Government borrowing and investment at the margin will replace private borrowing and investment, and total capital formation will not be affected.[8] On the other hand, if deficit-financed

---

[6] That is, if (1) government debt is viewed as wealth by its holders and not as a liability by taxpayers in general who will have to pay future interest on the debt, or (2) if the "wealth effect" on bondholders outweighs the "liability effect" on taxpayers.

[7] The reader interested in a more technical exposition of this discussion should consult Jerome Stein, "Unemployment, Inflation, and Monetarism," *American Economic Review*, vol. 64 (December 1974), and "Inside the Monetarist Black Box," mimeo. (November 2, 1974), along with James Tobin, "Long-run Effects of Fiscal and Monetary Policy on Aggregate Demand," Cowles Foundation Discussion Paper No. 384 (December 13, 1974). These papers also contain useful references to other work done on this problem.

[8] Martin J. Bailey, "The Optimum Full Employment Surplus," *Journal of Political Economy*, vol. 80 (July/August 1972). Paul A. David and John Scadding, "Private Savings: Ultrarationality, Aggregation and Denison's Law," *Journal of Political Economy*, vol. 82 (March/April 1974).

government expenditures are of the consumption variety, private borrowers will still be in the market, and federal borrowing will be more likely to crowd out private borrowing for capital expansion.

Thus, the impact of the fiscal stimulus on the overall level of aggregate demand will depend on the effect the resulting deficits have on consumption and on interest rates and whether consumers treat deficit-financed government expenditures as consumption-type or investment-type goods.

At present, empirical evidence of the relative impact of increases in wealth on consumption and on the demand for money, and the effect of government deficits on the demand for private investment, does not provide a clear-cut answer to the question of whether or not tax cuts and expenditure increases will increase total demand and output. However, it is possible to get some perspective on how serious the "crowding out" problem may be. The official projection by the CEA in February was that, with the President's fiscal program in effect, current-dollar GNP would be about $1,500 billion in 1975 and $1,686 billion in 1976. The CEA also projected gross private investment for 1975. Nonresidential fixed investment (in current dollars) was expected to rise by 4 percent in 1975 over 1974, inventories were expected to decline by $5 billion, and current-dollar residential construction was expected to be about $44 billion, down 5 percent from 1974. Thus, as Table 8 shows, with net foreign investment at −$5 billion, total gross investment to be financed would be about $190 billion in 1975.

What about gross savings? As Edward F. Denison [9] has pointed out, gross *private* saving—by businesses and consumers—has been an amazingly stable fraction of GNP. During the period 1948–73, it averaged 15.6 percent of GNP, with a maximum of 16.8 percent and a minimum of 14.5 percent. In 1974 it was 15.3 percent. Applying the average gross private saving ratio to predicted GNP in 1975 yields $234 of gross private saving. With a federal deficit—after the revisions in the original fiscal program (see Table 7)—of more than $76 billion, and assuming the state and local sector roughly in balance, total gross national saving (private saving minus the deficit) would be around $158 billion. This leaves us with a gap of $32 billion between gross investment and gross savings.

In order to avoid "crowding out" adequate room is needed for financing this shortage by means of monetary expansion. The increase

[9] Edward F. Denison, "A Note on Private Saving," *Review of Economics and Statistics*, vol. 40 (August 1958), pp. 261-67. See also David and Scadding, "Private Savings," and the references they cite.

Table 8

THE FEDERAL SECTOR DEFICIT AND THE SAVINGS-INVESTMENT BALANCE, CALENDAR YEARS 1975–76[a]

(current $ in billions)

Item	1975	1976
Gross private domestic investment (CEA forecast for 1975, authors' estimates for 1976)	195	267
Business fixed	156	183
Change in inventories	−5	15
Residential construction	44	69
Net foreign investment	−5	−5
Total, gross investment	190	262
Gross savings		
Gross private savings (15.6 percent of GNP)	234	263
Government sector deficit	−76	−65
Total, gross savings	158	198
Gap: excess of gross investment over gross savings	32	64
Monetary policy: required rate of growth in monetary base to fill gap	4.5%	8.0%

[a] NIA basis.

needed in the monetary base and in bank credit in order to create a market for the remainder of the government securities corresponding to the 1975 deficit is quite a bit smaller than the actual increase is likely to be. Indeed, it is quite a bit smaller than the increase in the monetary base and bank credit presumably implied in the various GNP forecasts, which nonetheless suggest a substantial reduction of inflation during the year. Thus, no "crowding out" is likely to occur. Moreover, to the extent that the extra $14 billion of fiscal stimulus (see Table 7) may generate extra GNP, additional gross savings will also be generated. For each $10 billion rise in GNP we might obtain about $2.4 billion of additional government revenue and $1.6 billion of gross private savings.[10] This further reduces the likelihood of any "crowding out" effect in 1975.

However, the real problem would be faced in 1976, when, in the event of the expected tendency toward a healthy recovery, failure of the deficit to decline significantly would seriously interfere with that

[10] This assumes an elasticity of federal revenues with respect to GNP of 1.2 and a level of private savings at 15.6 percent of GNP.

tendency. If, as now seems likely, the structural changes incorporated in the congressional tax bill are made permanent, the extra net fiscal stimulus provided in the newer fiscal program will be $25 billion more than the original budget for 1976 provided. (See the discussion of Table 7 above.) The CEA forecast was that GNP would rise 12.6 percent in calendar 1975 to $1,686 billion with the administration's original fiscal/energy program. However, 2 to 3 percentage points of that growth would have reflected the inflation due to the energy program that Congress has already rejected. Without the energy program the original forecast would thus presumably have implied an increase in GNP of perhaps 10 percent, to around $1,648 billion. On the other hand, the added fiscal stimulus should provide enough more real growth to achieve the estimated GNP of $1,686 billion. This would be consistent with gross private domestic investment of perhaps $267 billion (see Table 8). If net foreign investment were roughly constant between 1975 and 1976, gross investment would then total $272 billion in calendar 1976.

On the savings side, about $263 billion of gross private saving would be forthcoming at the forecasted level of GNP. With a balanced budget in the state-local sector and the federal deficit at $65 billion (Table 7), the shortfall of savings would then be $74 billion (Table 8). To fill the gap, the monetary base and bank credit would have to grow at a rate of about 8 percent in calendar 1976, *even* if appreciable additional credit-market strains developing from an increased demand for consumer loans could be disregarded, which, of course, can not be done. There is the further threat that budgetary actions by the Congress could raise the deficit in calendar 1976 even higher than is now projected. Unless outlays are kept sufficiently under control, interest rates will rise steeply and government spending *will* crowd out private spending. If in these circumstances the Federal Reserve should adopt inflationary policies in an attempt to keep interest rates from rising, it could achieve this objective at best only temporarily and at the cost of getting the economy into serious difficulties subsequently. Hence it is essential to work now toward a significant decrease of the deficit in the first year of the recovery.

The 1975 Tax Cuts. Table 9 shows the congressional tax cut bill for 1975–76 on a liability basis and by type of tax. As the table indicates, most of the tax relief—about $20 billion, or 71 percent of the tax cut in 1975—will accrue to individuals. Corporations will receive a tax cut of about $4.5 billion in 1975, which is partly offset by the increase in their taxes ($2 billion) due to the reduction of the deple-

Table 9

A SUMMARY OF THE CONGRESSIONAL TAX BILL, INDIVIDUALS AND BUSINESS, LIABILITY BASIS, CALENDAR YEAR 1975–76

($ in billions)

Item	1975	1976[a]
Relief for individuals, total	20.3	−8.3
Rebate against 1974 taxes	−8.1	0
Housing credit	−0.6	0
Exemption credit	−5.3	−5.3
Minimum and standard deduction	−2.5	−2.6
Earned income credit	−1.5	0
Child care deduction	−0.1	−0.1
Social care deduction	−1.7	0
Unemployment benefit liberalization	−0.2	0
Investment tax credit for individuals	−0.3	−0.3
Relief for business, net total	−2.5	−2.3
Corporate ITC	−3.0	−3.0
Corporate rate reduction	−1.5	−1.5
Repeal of the oil depletion	1.6	1.6
Foreign source income	0.4	0.6
Total net reduction in liabilities	−23.8	−10.6

[a] Assuming that the minimum and standard deductions and exemption credit provisions are made permanent. The child care deduction is permanent, and the investment tax credit extends through 1976.

Source: U.S. Treasury and authors' estimates.

tion allowance and the changes in the tax treatment of foreign sources of income.

To analyze the impact of these provisions on the economy, we will begin first with those changes that affect individuals. Since the bill contains several types of provisions—rebates and structural changes—these will be discussed separately in terms of (1) whether the change is temporary or permanent and (2) what effect these changes will have on the distribution of the tax burden among various income classes. Next the effect of the tax cut for business will be examined both in terms of its stimulatory effect on the economy and the distribution of the relief by income class.

Individual tax relief. Economists generally agree that the effect of tax cuts on private spending, at least in the short run, depends upon the type of tax cut—temporary or permanent—and upon the distribution of the relief by income class.

On a theoretical level, a permanent tax cut affects "permanent" aftertax income and thus permanent consumption. On the other hand, a temporary tax cut is treated as transitory change in income and thus, it is argued, has little impact on the consumption behavior of households. However, some empirical studies have concluded that even if the temporary tax cut is treated as a windfall gain, it will lead to a significant increase in consumption, especially on such items as durables.[11] Other studies show a low correlation between windfall gains and increased consumption,[12] thus leaving us with conflicting evidence on the subject. However, the weight of opinion, if not firm empirical evidence, suggests that, per dollar, a permanent tax cut will affect consumption more than will a temporary tax cut.

Another way to look at this issue is to note that a permanent tax cut not only increases "take-home pay" in this period, but also increases anticipated take-home pay in future periods as well. It seems likely that this increase in the consumers' present and future expected income stream would induce a much larger amount of consumption per dollar of tax relief than would a temporary tax cut (such as the tax rebates provided for in the President's tax/energy proposal and in the congressional tax bill) treated as a windfall gain.

The distribution of the tax-cut benefits, regardless of whether they are permanent or temporary, affects the total amount of consumption induced if families in different income classes have different propensities to consume. Since it is the general belief that lower-income families consume more of each additional dollar received, a tax package which targets most of the relief toward lower-income families will produce a greater impact than one of equal size which spreads the benefits more evenly among all income groups.

However, Robert C. Jones's study throws some doubt on the argument's relevance to the present situation.[13] Dividing "windfall" income recipients into two income groups, Jones found a lower propensity among lower-income recipients to consume "windfall" income

---

[11] Ronald Bodkin's study shows that the marginal propensity to consume out of windfall gains is somewhere between 0.72 and 0.97 ("Windfall Income and Consumption," *American Economic Review*, September 1959). See also, Robert C. Jones, "Transitory Income and Expenditure on Consumption Categories," *American Economic Review*, May 1960, and C. Bird, "Consumption, Savings and Windfall Gains: Comment," *American Economic Review*, June 1965.

[12] M. E. Kreinin, "Windfall Income and Consumption—Additional Evidence," *American Economic Review*, June 1961; and Margaret Reid, "Consumption, Savings and Windfall Gains: Reply," *American Economic Review*, June 1963.

[13] Jones, "Transitory Income and Expenditures," pp. 584-92.

as opposed to other income by spending it on housing and clothing. The coefficient for food, however, was highest in the lower-income group, as was the coefficient for housing, clothing, and food considered together. At a time when the durable consumer goods and housing sectors are those hardest hit by recession, while retail food prices and demand have just peaked and the industry does not yet show slack, it seems likely that a small tax rebate concentrated in the low-income groups will result in additional expenditures and demand largely in the food industry. This could lead to renewed pressure on prices, while giving little if any relief to the depressed durable goods and housing markets, especially since a large proportion of all purchases of consumer durables and houses is concentrated in the $20,000-50,000 income classes.

In this regard, the rebate in the congressional bill—an average of about $100 and a maximum of $200—which gives 90 percent of the relief to taxpayers with annual incomes of less than $20,000 (see (Table 10) is less desirable than the administration version (see Table 10). The administration's version spreads the rebate over all income levels with an average rebate of $150 (a maximum of $1,000), and provides about $6 billion of relief to taxpayers in the critical $20,000-50,000 range. However, since the congressional bill provides a credit toward housing purchases, this, in addition to the rebate, should help housing and related industries. Yet, although it is beneficial to the housing industry, the housing credit may further distort the relationship of the sector to other sectors in the economy. Because the corporate income tax does not fall on housing and because of the relatively preferable tax treatment of the housing sector under the personal income tax, capital in the corporate sector has been discriminated against as compared to the housing sector. The additional preference introduced by the credit will further increase the differential in the tax treatment of the two sectors and will increase the welfare loss due to the tax-induced misallocation of resources between sectors.[14]

The distributional impact of the permanent changes provided in the tax bill, as compared with those in the present law, is shown in Table 11. These are the changes in the minimum standard deduction,

---

[14] For more detail on this point, see David J. Ott and Attiat F. Ott, "The Effect of Non-neutral Taxation on the Use of Capital by Sector," *Journal of Political Economy*, July/August 1973. The distributional aspects of the social security bonus and the increase in unemployment benefits, because they accrue mostly to nonfilers and are in the nature of welfare payments rather than tax relief, will not be discussed here.

Table 10

DISTRIBUTIONAL IMPACT OF THE ADMINISTRATION'S REBATE PROPOSAL, AS COMPARED TO THE CONGRESSIONAL BILL, CALENDAR YEAR 1975

Adjusted Gross Income Class ($ thousands)	Number of Returns ($ millions)	Adjusted Gross Income ($ millions)	Taxable Income ($ millions)	Present Law Taxes ($ millions)	Administration Proposal		Congressional Bill	
					Amount of tax change ($ millions)	Tax change per return (dollars)	Amount of tax change ($ millions)	Tax change per return (dollars)
0-3	17.80	22,297	1,788	283	−30	−2	−230	−13
3-5	9.00	35,346	11,658	1,778	−213	−24	−685	−76
5-7	8.60	51,264	24,992	4,092	−491	−57	−795	−92
7-10	11.70	98,825	54,091	9,251	−1,110	−95	−1,197	−102
10-15	16.10	198,536	118,384	21,239	−2,549	−158	−2,178	−135
15-20	9.90	169,929	109,740	20,910	−2,509	−253	−1,796	−181
20-50	9.00	241,778	170,423	38,417	−4,489	−499	−1,162	−129
50-100	0.66	44,002	34,136	11,875	−647	−980	−65	−98
100 and over	0.16	28,880	21,886	10,952	−158	−987	−16	−100

Source: U.S. Treasury Department; tax data are on a liabilities basis, using 1974 tax model.

Table 11

DISTRIBUTIONAL EFFECT OF THREE TAX-CUT PROVISIONS[a]

(estimated revenue effect at 1974 income levels)

Adjusted Gross Income Class ($ thousands)	Taxes under Present Law ($ millions)	Number of Returns Made Nontaxable ($ thousands)	Number of Returns with Tax Decrease ($ thousands)	Amount of Tax Decrease ($ millions)	Tax Decrease as a Percent of Taxes Paid
0-3	283	2,408	5,186	−454	160.0[b]
3-5	1,778	1,744	8,412	−1,273	72.0
5-7	4,092	1,351	8,526	−1,339	33.0
7-10	9,251	491	11,534	−1,451	16.0
10-15	21,239	84	15,952	−1,804	8.0
15-20	20,910	12	9,856	−1,426	7.0
20-50	38,417	4	9,006	−1,180	1.0
50-100	11,875	—	655	−80	0.7
100 and over	10,952	[a]	160	−18	0.2
Total	118,800	6,093	69,286	−9,032	

[a] These provisions are: the increase in the minimum and percentage standard deductions, the exemption credit, and the earned income credit.

[b] For the first income class, the tax cut exceeds present law taxes due to the refundable earned income credit.

Source: U.S. Treasury tax model.

the standard deduction, the exemption credit, and the earned income credit.

The effects of these provisions, shown in Tables 11 and 12, point to the fact that the congressional bill concentrates its relief in the first three income brackets, where the relief more than wipes out taxes for households with incomes up to $3,000. As income rises, the relief declines to 1 percent in the $20,000-50,000 income classes. These changes, if they become permanent, would alter appreciably the distribution of the personal income tax burden among income classes. As Table 12 shows, the effect of these three provisions is to lower dramatically the share of taxes paid by households with incomes below $7,000, reduce it moderately for other households with incomes below $15,000, and to increase the share paid by those with incomes above $15,000. Furthermore, the largest percentage point increase is concentrated in the $20,000-50,000 income class.

Given the fact that it is estimated that 18 million out of a total of 82 million taxpayers will pay about 50 percent of total individual income taxes collected by the federal government in 1975, the pattern of burden distribution that emerges under the congressional bill adds

Table 12

EFFECT OF THE CONGRESSIONAL TAX BILL ON EFFECTIVE TAX RATE AND TAXES PAID, BY ADJUSTED GROSS INCOME CLASS[a]

Adjusted Gross Income Class ($ thousands)	**Effective Rate under Present Law** (percent)	**Effective Rate under Congressional Tax Bill** (percent)	**Taxes as a Percent of Taxes Paid, by Income Class under Present Law**	**Taxes as a Percent of Taxes Paid, by Income Class under the Bill**
0-3	1	b	0.2	b
3-5	5	1.0	1.5	0.4
5-7	8	5.0	3.4	2.5
7-10	9	7.9	7.8	7.0
10-15	10	9.7	17.9	17.7
15-20	12	11.4	17.6	17.7
20-50	16	15.4	32.3	33.9
50-100	27	26.8	10.0	10.7
100 and over	38	37.9	9.2	9.9

[a] Includes only the effects of the increase in the minimum and standard deduction, the exemption credit, and the earned income credit.

[b] The effective tax rate is negative due to the refundable earned income credit.

Source: U.S. Treasury estimates at 1974 income levels.

further to the strain on these taxpayers, particularly those in this group for whom work is the major source of income. Future increases in tax rates will be excessively burdensome on these groups, since the further reduction in the number of persons paying tax, and thus the tax base, means that such increases will again fall heavily on the 18 million. At a time when an improvement in productivity is essential for economic growth, saddling one of the more productive groups in the economy with an additional tax burden to finance more benefit payments would seem to be unproductive.

The three remaining provisions of the tax bill—the $50 cash payment to social security recipients, the earned income credit, and the increased benefits to the unemployed—represent a departure from the previous practice of separating the income tax system from the income maintenance system. If the tax system is to be used to provide income maintenance for the poor, the changes must be carefully considered for their impact on work incentives and in conjunction with changes in other welfare programs, which was not done in the case of the congressional bill. In terms of impact on the economy, these provisions clearly fall in the "windfall" gain category. The receipts are likely to be spent on food and related items without providing any major stimulus to the depressed durable goods markets.

Business tax cuts. In addition to providing tax relief to individuals, the congressional tax bill contains several provisions which will alter the effective tax rate on corporate income. Provisions which will reduce the effective tax rate include: an increase in the investment tax credit from 7 percent to 10 percent, and a redefinition of normal income as the first $50,000 (rather than the present $25,000) of corporate income, with the rate of tax on the first $25,000 being reduced from 22 percent to 20 percent. In sum, these provisions are expected to lower the effective tax rate on corporate profits by 3 percentage points (8.5 percent), from about 39 percent to 36 percent.

Provisions that increase the effective tax rate on corporate income do so to the extent that corporations have income from foreign sources and/or derive their income from oil. The repeal of the depletion write-off for major oil companies and the increase in U.S. taxes on the foreign income of multinational companies will add back 1.5 percentage points, raising the effective tax rate on those corporations from 36 percent to 37.5 percent, leaving a net tax relief to oil companies as a group of 1.5 percentage points.[15]

[15] Provisions that have less of an effect on business include the elimination of special export tax breaks for petroleum and the use of the investment tax credit for drilling rigs used outside North America.

In evaluating these tax changes, one must distinguish between effects on incentives and effects on the overall distribution of the tax burden. By reducing the effective corporate tax rate, the tax cut will lead to an increase in the aftertax rate of return on corporate investment and will thus stimulate further investment and capital accumulation. The investment tax credit—which reduces the rental price of capital—is expected to have a large impact on capital formation. It is estimated that investment increases by 6.8 percent for every one percentage point increase in the investment tax credit.[16] This suggests that, at the 1974 level of investment in producers' durable goods, raising the investment tax credit by three percentage points will add about $14 billion to corporate investment. However, given the relative increase in the effective tax rate on oil companies vis-à-vis other corporations, some distortion in the allocation of corporate capital may take place. In fact, repealing the depletion allowance and increasing the effective tax rate on foreign-source income, without deregulating oil and natural gas prices, will frustrate the objective of reducing reliance on foreign sources of oil and gas by causing a reduction in exploration and investment in the U.S. oil and gas industry.

The effect of the business tax cuts on the relative distribution of federal income taxes between individuals and corporations can be determined by comparing the effect of the corporate tax cut with that of the reduction in the individual income tax. As is shown in Table 12, the overall effective tax rate on individuals for 1975 was reduced from 13.3 percent to 12.3 percent by the congressional tax bill. For corporations (excluding oil companies) the rate was cut from 39 percent to 36 percent. (The net rate cut, as noted above, was 1.5 percentage points for oil companies.)

When corporate income and the corporate tax reduction are imputed to stockholders, the inequitable pattern of the distribution of relief discussed earlier is further intensified, as is shown in Table 13. Here again one income class—in this case those with incomes between $20,000 and $50,000—is discriminated against under the new tax bill, their taxes being reduced least.

In short, although the tax bill has merit in terms of its likely impact on capital formation and the stimulation of aggregate demand, it ranks low in terms of its neutrality (housing market vis-à-vis other sectors), work incentives, and equity in the distribution of the tax burden.

---

[16] Charles W. Bischoff, "Business Investment in the 1970's: A Comparison of Models," *Brookings Papers on Economic Activity*, no. 1 (1971), pp. 13-58.

Table 13

EFFECT ON TAX LIABILITY OF THE COMBINED TAX CUT FOR INDIVIDUALS AND CORPORATIONS, BY ADJUSTED GROSS INCOME CLASS[a]

Adjusted Gross Income Class ($ thousands)	**Amount of Tax Reduction**[b] ($ millions)	**Tax Reduction as a Percent of Taxes Paid**
0-5	−1,727	84
5-7	−1,377	34
7-10	−1,526	16
10-15	−1,929	9
15-20	−1,613	8
20-50	−1,638	4
50 and over	−1,386	6
Total	−11,195	—

[a] Tax cuts for individuals of $9.0 billion include the increase in the minimum and percentage standard deduction, the $30 exemption credit and the earned income credit. Corporate tax reductions of $2.5 billion is the net reduction.

[b] Corporate tax reduction is allocated according to ownership of corporate stock.

Source: U.S. Treasury Department and authors' estimates.

The Timing of the Fiscal Stimulus. A further consideration in evaluating the original administration proposal and the congressional alternative is the timing of the stimulus they provide to the economy. Given the expectation that the economy will "bottom out" by the middle of 1975 and then begin a recovery, and given the lag in the response of the economy to either fiscal or monetary stimulus, it would seem appropriate to try to provide as much of the stimulus as possible in the first half of 1975. If the stimulus comes later its impact may—because of lags—not be felt until the economy is already recovering, rather than preceding and stimulating the recovery.

Table 14 compares the path of stimulus for 1975 under the administration's tax/energy program with that under the congressional alternative. (It is assumed that, whatever the final form of the congressional energy program, it will be a "wash" in the aggregate. That is, it is assumed that any excess receipts from energy taxes will be offset by increases in expenditures.)

The top bank of figures in Table 14 shows the net stimulus (the effect on the full-employment surplus) of the two proposals, assuming that rebates under the administration plan would be paid

Table 14

TIMING OF NET STIMULUS UNDER THE ADMINISTRATION'S TAX/ENERGY PROPOSAL AND THE CONGRESSIONAL BILL DURING 1975 AND THE FIRST HALF OF 1976[a]

(current $ in billions, seasonally adjusted to annual rates)

	1975				1976	
Item	I	II	III	IV	I	II
Net stimulus						
(1) Administration proposal	−0.3	−8.2	−51.7	−17.1	−6.3	−4.0
(2) Congressional bill	−2.8	−51.9	−17.5	−17.5	−11.2	−11.4
Difference: (2) minus (1)[b]	−2.5	−43.7	34.2	−0.4	−4.9	−7.4
Net stimulus with rebates paid in 1974-II						
(1) Administration proposal	−0.3	−36.5	−22.5	−17.1	c	c
(2) Congressional bill	−2.8	−51.9	−17.5	−17.5	c	c
Difference: (2) minus (1)[b]	−2.5	−15.4	5.0	−0.4	c	c

[a] NIA basis.

[b] (−) means that the congressional bill is more stimulatory and (+) means that the administration proposal is more stimulatory.

[c] Same as above—no effect on 1976 path.

Source: U.S. Department of Commerce, Bureau of Economic Analysis, and authors' estimates.

in May and September 1975), as proposed, while under the congressional alternative, rebates would be paid in May. Although the administration proposal would have put most of the stimulus in the third quarter of 1975 (roughly two-thirds of all of its calendar year 1975 stimulus would have fallen within this period), the congressional tax cut and spending increases are concentrated in the second quarter of 1975.

Given the economic forecast for 1975, it is appropriate to apply—as the congressional bill does—much of the stimulus as early as possible. This enables the stimulus to help the economy toward recovery without exerting excessive pressure on prices and interest rates.

However, the duration of the stimulus provided by the congressional bill is somewhat unclear. Although the bill provides for some fundamental changes in the structure of the personal income tax—the increase in the minimum standard and in the percentage standard deductions, the exemption credit, and the earned income credit—it is unclear whether such changes are to be permanent or are meant solely to apply to 1975 tax liability. Conflicting reports emerge as to the permanency of such changes. Commenting on the congressional bill, the *Wall Street Journal* speculated that "the conference went along with a $7.8 billion tax cut (for 1975) but only for this year." [17] However, the same newspaper reported that "all the individual cuts technically are for this year only, although there undoubtedly will be moves to make some of them permanent." [18] The permanency of the changes in the tax structure implied in the $7.8 billion figure quoted from the *Wall Street Journal* seems most likely. The $7.8 billion is the price tag for increasing the value of the minimum and percentage standard deductions ($2.5 billion) and the exemption credit ($5.3 billion). The history of tax legislation would seem to point to either retention of the changes in both the minimum and percentage standard deductions, or even, perhaps, to an increase in the future.

A more significant change is the exemption credit. For several years, proposals to reform the federal income tax system have contained provisions for converting the existing system of personal exemptions to an exemption credit. The congressional bill's provision for a $30 credit per exemption is a "foot in the door" toward this alternative, and thus it seems more likely now than ever before that this provision will be retained and perhaps strengthened in the future.

The earned-income credit, although not considered as strong a candidate for permanency, seems likely to achieve it. This provision constitutes a "first" in the history of the personal income tax system; the negative income tax concept has in effect been adopted. It may well become permanent as a way of integrating the positive with a negative income tax system.

Thus, if some or all of these features of the congressional bill become permanent, the stimulus of this part of the bill would continue through succeeding years. In the first half of 1976, these features would provide stimulus of roughly $11 billion (annual rate). This illustrates a basic dilemma in using tax cuts as a stimulatory tool. If, as was discussed earlier, a "permanent" tax cut has a greater impact than a one-time windfall gain, then it is clearly to be preferred to a rebate or a temporary tax cut from the standpoint of obtaining

---

[17] *Wall Street Journal*, March 27, 1975, p. 3.

[18] Ibid.

a greater stimulatory effect. On the other hand, the very fact that it *is* permanent makes such a tax cut continue its stimulus beyond the period when it is needed. In 1976, if stimulus is no longer desired, the lower path of personal and corporate taxes will require offsetting cuts in expenditures or some form of tax increases.

If the administration's rebates had been paid in full in the second quarter of 1975, as is shown in the lower bank of figures in Table 14, this would have concentrated the net stimulus much more in the period before the recovery is supposed to begin—with less risk of undesirable effects from the deficit than would result if the rebate payments were spread out. However, the congressional bill is still more stimulatory in every quarter except the third than is the administration program. Its major defect is that substantial stimulus may continue into 1976 and beyond as a result of retaining the structural changes. This long-run aspect will be discussed further in Section 4.

The Behavior of the State-Local Sector. There are some plausible theoretical arguments and some evidence suggesting that the state and local sector behaves perversely in providing discretionary fiscal stimulus during a recession. State and local governments must usually operate on balanced budgets on current accounts, although they borrow to finance some capital expenditures. As the economy declines and their revenues from personal and corporate income taxes (and to a lesser degree from sales and excise taxes) decline, they must raise tax rates or restrain expenditure growth in order to maintain a balanced current account. At the local level, property taxes bear the brunt of the upward rate adjustments; at the state level, rates for either income or sales taxes, or both, may be raised to eliminate the impending deficit.

The 1974 *Report of the Council of Economic Advisers*, in presenting estimates of the full-employment surplus of state and local governments, took note of the possible perversity argument on the tax side but did not account for it in their estimates.

> There is also some evidence that [state and local] tax rates tend to be raised when the gap between actual GNP and potential GNP widens. *The average tax rates at full employment may therefore deviate systematically from the actual tax rates, contrary to the assumption made in estimating full employment receipts.* [Emphasis added.] [19]

[19] *Report of the Council of Economic Advisers*, p. 81.

In an unpublished paper, R. C. Vogel has shown that, on the receipt side, there is substance to the perversity argument:

> . . . the present findings also reveal that state and local governments raise their tax rates in an effort to offset shortfalls in receipts when actual GNP fails to reach potential, so that, state and local governments are in fact cyclically perverse.[20]

Moreover, he finds the tax rate response to economic decline to be rather rapid, occurring over one or two quarters.[21] This leads him to suggest that attempts by the federal government to provide fiscal stimulus might well include increases in grants-in-aid to "forestall offsetting increases in state and local tax rates when actual GNP falls short of potential." The President's tax/energy program does contain a proposal to increase general revenue sharing grants by $2 billion. However, this would merely offset increased costs at the state and local levels and would not forestall the tax-expenditure perversity in state-local budget behavior, which would negate some of the proposed fiscal stimulus. The House plan contains no suggestions for increased grants.

Thus, as the 1975 Council of Economic Advisers report notes:

> Budgetary reserves are now so tight that the rise in state and local expenditures will have to slow considerably to adjust to the reduced growth of receipts, or taxes will have to be raised in a declining economy. The full employment surplus of state and local governments that held fairly steady in 1973 and in the first half of 1974 *is thus expected to rise sharply in 1975.* [Emphasis added.] [22]

In light of these conclusions, it seems somewhat incongruous that neither the administration plan nor the congressional alternatives, at this writing, include a temporary increase in grants as part of their program of providing the fiscal stimulus.

4. The Long-Run Budget Outlook

The budget for fiscal year 1976 was the first one submitted by the Ford administration. As was noted in the foregoing section, the short-

---

[20] R. C. Vogel, "The Responsiveness of State and Local Receipts to Changes in Economic Activity: Extending the Concept of the Full Employment Budget," mimeo. (1974), p. 24.

[21] Ibid., p. 15.

[22] *Report of the Council of Economic Advisers* (Washington, D. C.: Government Printing Office, 1975), p. 65.

run thrust of the original budget program, as well as the modifications made since it was submitted to Congress, have centered around providing fiscal stimulus to aid in promoting economic recovery. But what about the long run? What are the implications of the fiscal 1976 budget, and subsequent changes in it, for the balance in the federal budget when full employment is reached? In particular, what will be the long-run impact of the tax changes made in 1975? In this section, we will discuss the long-term outlook under both the administration's original fiscal 1976 budget program and the budget program resulting from subsequent actions by the Congress and the administration.

The Federal Budget Outlook. Table 15 projects budget outlays for fiscal years 1977–82 under programs and initiatives in the Ford administration's proposed fiscal 1976 budget.[23] It shows the path of projected budget outlays under the following assumptions about the rate of inflation and the path of unemployment: the private GNP deflator rises 10.5 percent in 1975, 6 percent in 1976, and 4 percent each year from 1977 through 1981, while the rate of unemployment averages 8.5 percent in 1975, 6 percent in 1976, and 4.7 percent thereafter.[24] This does not imply that the rate of inflation is forecast to be 4 percent by 1977 or that the unemployment rate will in fact be brought down to 4.7 percent. It is certainly, for example, a more optimistic scenario than the one set out in the fiscal 1976 budget, where the rate of inflation does not subside to 4 percent until 1980 and the unemployment rate drops only to 5.5 percent—and then only by 1980. However, the above assumptions were made because our objective is to project the budget path at full employment and a more acceptable rate of inflation than was experienced during 1973 and 1974.

---

[23] To facilitate the expenditure projections, the "old" (July 1–June 30) fiscal years were used rather than the new October 1–September 30 fiscal year which will go into effect with fiscal year 1977. The outlays shown in Table 15 are thus not comparable with the official fiscal year projections shown in the fiscal 1976 budget.

[24] The projections also assume that output per man-hour rises at a rate of 2.9 percent a year over the projection period and that the labor force grows with Census Series E projections. See Dennis F. Johnston, "U.S. Labor Force: Projections through 1990," *Monthly Labor Review*, December 1973. The full-employment surplus is based on the assumption of a "global" unemployment rate of 4.7 percent, rather than the 4.0 percent that was conventional in the 1960s and early 1970s. Most labor market analysts agree that 4.7 percent now represents a more realistic measure of full employment, given changes in the structure of the labor force since the mid-fifties.

Table 15

PROJECTED UNIFIED BUDGET OF THE ADMINISTRATION: FEDERAL OUTLAYS, BY FUNCTION, AND PROJECTED OUTLAYS AFTER EXPENDITURE CHANGES, FISCAL YEARS 1977–82

(current $ in billions)

Functional Code and Title		Fiscal Year						
		1976	1977	1978	1979	1980	1981	1982
050	National defense	94	101	106	114	121	129	138
150	International affairs	6	8	8	8	8	8	8
250	General science, space and technology	5	5	5	5	5	5	4
300	Natural resources, environment, and energy	10	12	14	14	15	16	16
350	Agriculture	2	2	2	2	3	3	3
400	Commerce and transportation	15	16	16	17	18	19	20
450	Community and regional development	6	6	7	6	6	6	7
500	Education, manpower, and social services	15	16	16	17	18	19	20
550	Health	29	31	35	40	45	50	56
600	Income security	123	126	135	147	159	173	188
700	Veterans	16	16	16	16	17	17	17
750	Law enforcement and justice	3	4	4	4	4	5	5
800	General government	3	3	4	4	4	4	5
850	Revenue sharing and general purpose fiscal assistance	7	8	8	9	9	10	10
900	Interest	34	34	34	34	34	35	37
	Allowances and undistributed items	−10	−11	−12	−12	−13	−15	−16
	Total outlays, administration budget	355	373	394	421	449	480	514
	Changes in outlays	3	4	5	5	5	6	6
	Total	358	377	399	426	454	486	520

Source: BRAP estimates.

Table 15 shows projected outlays, by function, in fiscal years 1977–82 for the administration budget and the change in total outlays resulting from Congress's rejection of the administration's energy program and refusal to accept the proposed $11 billion of deferrals and recisions for fiscal 1976. Estimates of outlays were built up from separate projections of the *real* path of outlays, by type, for individual programs. That is, for each program area estimates were made of outlay levels in each fiscal year, assuming that prices remained at the same level as in fiscal year 1976. The estimates were based on projected caseloads, average *real* benefits, and so on, as set out in the fiscal 1976 budget document. The 1974 American Enterprise Institute Budget and Resource Allocation Projection (AEI-BRAP) model then generated total *current* dollar outlays and current dollar outlays for each functional category, given the inflation assumption. The projections of the administration budget assume enactment of the proposals in the fiscal 1976 budget for the energy/tax-rebate program, as well as significant increases in defense spending, but they do not assume the fiscal 1976 expenditure hold-downs of $6 billion under the "5-percent ceiling," since this proposal was rejected almost immediately after the original budget was submitted. They also do not assume that the large recession-induced outlays in fiscal 1976 for unemployment benefits and public employment will continue in the long run.

Converting the outlay projections to a national income accounts basis and to calendar years (1977–81) yields NIA federal sector expenditures. These are shown by NIA category in Table 16 for (1) the administration program, and (2) after the congressional actions on expenditures and taxes, along with the NIA federal sector full-employment receipts generated in each case by the 1975 AEI-BRAP model. Also shown is the full-employment surplus (that is, with a 4.7 percent unemployment rate) for the federal sector.

Table 16 indicates that we may have come full circle in the long-run budget outlook. Given the inflation and unemployment assumptions, under both the original administration budget and under the budget as since modified, the federal sector shows a deficit at full employment through 1977 and rough balance in 1978. The deficit is initially larger under the alternative budget because of congressional rejection of expenditure cuts and their larger and more permanent individual tax cut. However, after 1978 the congressional alternative shows roughly equal surpluses as the retention of the corporate surtax at 48 percent takes hold.

In 1972 there was considerable concern that the programs and policies set forth in the fiscal 1973 budget of the Nixon administration would result in budget deficits through 1976, even when measured at full employment.[25] In the fiscal 1974 budget, submitted in January 1973, the Nixon administration proposed holding down fiscal 1973 spending and a fiscal 1974 budget that would show a modest $4 billion surplus in the full-employment budget. Because the restraint on spending was attained, and because full-employment revenues turned out to be sharply higher—due mostly to higher offshore oil rents and royalties—than were anticipated, the fiscal year 1974 budget turned out to show a full-employment surplus of $9.7 billion.[26]

So the forward momentum of federal outlays was slowed by congressional and executive action in 1973 and 1974. As was indicated in a previous Long-Range Budget Projection (LRBP) project study, this turnaround in the rate of growth of expenditures laid the groundwork for a balanced full-employment budget in 1975, even without unexpectedly high rates of inflation and continued growth in oil revenues.[27] But now we have in effect come back to the original problem. The expenditure and tax programs embodied in the fiscal 1976 budget, as of this writing, have committed all federal revenues through 1978, even if full employment is restored, and there is only a slim margin of receipts over expenditures in 1979.

The Budget Outlook for State and Local Government. In previous LRBP studies, large and growing surpluses in the state and local sector had been projected for the last part of the 1970s.[28] However, these projections were quite crude. In particular, they showed a state-local sector surplus, on the assumption that not only would state-local tax receipts respond to increases in the tax base but that tax *rates* would continue to rise at the pace of the fifties and sixties. No effort was made to separate the behavior of state and local trust funds and general government accounts.

---

[25] See Charles L. Schultze, Edward R. Fried, Alice M. Rivlin, and Nancy H. Teeters, *Setting National Priorities: The 1973 Budget* (Washington, D. C.: The Brookings Institution, 1972), and David J. Ott et al., *Nixon, McGovern and the Federal Budget* (Washington, D. C.: American Enterprise Institute, 1972).

[26] Joint Statement of William E. Simon, Secretary of the Treasury, and Roy L. Ash, Director of the Office of Management and Budget, on Budget Results for Fiscal Year 1974 (July 24, 1974, processed).

[27] David J. Ott et al., *Public Claims on U.S. Output: Federal Budget Options in the Last Half of the Seventies* (Washington, D. C.: American Enterprise Institute, 1973).

[28] See Ott et al., *Nixon, McGovern and the Federal Budget* and *Public Claims on U.S. Output.*

Table 16

PROJECTED FEDERAL RECEIPTS, EXPENDITURES, AND SURPLUS OR DEFICIT, UNDER FISCAL YEAR 1976 BUDGET PROGRAM, FULL-EMPLOYMENT BASIS, 1977–81[a]

(current $ in billions)

Item	1977	1978	1979	1980	1981
ADMINISTRATION'S BUDGET					
Receipts					
Personal tax and nontax receipts	173	188	206	224	242
Contributions for social insurance	114	124	137	159	180
Corporate tax accruals	51	54	58	63	68
Indirect business taxes	55	53	57	60	60
Total receipts	393	419	459	506	554
Expenditures					
Purchases of goods and services	154	162	171	182	194
Defense	96	101	108	115	123
Other	58	60	63	67	71
Transfer payments	165	180	196	214	233
To persons	161	176	192	210	229
To foreigners	4	4	4	4	4
Grants to state and local governments	55	57	59	63	66
Subsidies less surpluses of government enterprises	4	4	4	4	4
Net interest paid	19	19	18	17	16
Total expenditures	397	421	449	480	513
Full-employment surplus or deficit (−)	−3	−2	9	27	41

Item	1977	1978	1979	1980	1981
CONGRESSIONAL ALTERNATIVE					
Receipts					
Personal tax and nontax receipts	185	201	220	239	259
Contributions for social insurance	114	124	137	159	180
Corporate tax accruals	62	66	71	77	83
Indirect business taxes	32	34	37	39	41
Total receipts	393	425	465	514	563
Expenditures					
Purchases of goods and services	152	161	170	181	193
Defense	96	101	108	115	123
Other	56	60	62	66	70
Transfer payments	167	182	199	217	236
To persons	163	178	195	213	232
To foreigners	4	4	4	4	4
Grants to state and local governments	58	60	63	66	70
Subsidies less surpluses of government enterprises	4	4	4	4	4
Net interest paid	19	19	18	17	17
Total expenditures	401	426	454	486	519
Full-employment surplus or deficit (−)	−8	−1	11	29	43

[a] NIA basis.

Note: Details may not add to totals because of rounding.

Source: BRAP estimates.

In a recent volume in the LRBP series, a more detailed analysis was made of the budget outlook for the state-local sector.[29] Separate models were developed for general government accounts and the trust funds, and they were integrated with the AEI-BRAP model to make the projections shown here. The details of the results are shown in the other volume and will not be repeated here. To summarize, however, the general pattern of large and growing state and local surpluses was confirmed, although the magnitudes were smaller than was suggested by the earlier, cruder model. With the current budget outlook (after congressional action on the administration's original budget), state and local governments are projected to run surpluses of $12 billion in 1977, growing thereafter to $16 billion by 1981 (see Table 17). The main forces producing the surplus are slowdowns in the growth of state and local construction, reflecting mainly demographic factors and the virtual completion of the interstate highway program coupled with rapid increases in federal grants for construction (thus necessitating less borrowing and a smaller deficit), together with continued sizable trust fund surpluses. The analysis also suggests that, aside from the pattern of surpluses, the state and local sector as a whole will be able to meet its objectives without increasing tax rates, or, at worst, with small rate increases that are in no way comparable to those of the fifties and sixties.

Finally, it should again be stressed that this brighter fiscal outlook for the sector as a whole does not imply a similar picture for each and every state and local unit. Some units will still be hard-pressed financially, and a concern of future federal grants-in-aid policy will probably be to identify these governmental units and target new aid to them, without weakening their own incentives to tackle local problems. When general revenue sharing is considered for renewal in 1975, the discussion might well focus on revamping the formula by which funds are allocated to states and localities to provide new assurance that it is aimed more toward the most needy units.

The Federal Budget and Claims on GNP. Suppose that by 1977 the assumptions used here are in fact realized, that the rate of inflation can be brought down to 4 percent a year, with a 4.7 percent unemployment rate and with the long-run posture described here for the federal budget actually attained. What would be the balance between

---

[29] David J. Ott, Attiat F. Ott, James A. Maxwell, and F. Richard Aronson, *State-Local Finances in the Last Half of the 1970s* (Washington, D. C.: American Enterprise Institute, 1975).

Table 17

PROJECTED RECEIPTS, EXPENDITURES, AND SURPLUS IN THE STATE AND LOCAL SECTOR UNDER THE FISCAL YEAR 1976 BUDGET AS MODIFIED BY CONGRESS, 1977–81[a]

(current $ in billions)

Item	1977	1978	1979	1980	1981
Receipts	328	374	416	469	524
Expenditures	316	363	404	455	509
Surplus	12	11	12	14	16

[a] NIA basis.

Note: Details may not add to totals because of rounding.

Source: BRAP estimates.

Table 18

PROJECTED GROSS NATIONAL PRODUCT, FINAL DEMAND, AND THE GAP, UNDER THE FISCAL YEAR 1976 BUDGET AS MODIFIED BY CONGRESS, 1977–81[a]

(current $ in billions)

Item	1977	1978	1979	1980	1981
Gross National Product	2001	2170	2356	2552	2750
Consumption	1220	1304	1398	1486	1574
Business fixed investment	228	247	267	289	311
Inventory investment	22	24	26	28	30
Residential construction	89	92	101	106	115
Net exports	0	0	0	0	0
Federal purchases	152	161	170	181	193
Defense	96	101	108	115	123
Other	57	59	62	66	71
State and local purchases	318	361	399	443	489
Final demand	2029	2189	2361	2532	2711
Gap (excess of final demand over GNP)	28	19	5	−20	−39

[a] NIA basis.

Note: Details may not add to totals because of rounding.

Source: BRAP estimates.

total output and final demand? How much room would there be for the extra investment some writers have seen as necessary in order to adjust to higher environmental standards and the energy crisis?[30] What room would there be for federal tax cuts or spending increases on new program initiatives or on existing programs? Table 18 provides a basis for discussing these questions. It shows GNP, final demand, and the "gap"—the excess of final demand over GNP—in current prices, assuming that the gross private savings rate is 15.6 percent of GNP and that the United States manages to balance its foreign trade account.

With these assumptions, there is an excess of final demand over GNP through 1979; the excess of demand over output (in current dollars) is $28 billion in 1977, falls to $5 billion by 1979, and is below GNP only in 1980. This suggests that the "crowding out" problem discussed above may be of concern through 1977 at least, unless the federal deficit is reduced by tax increases or expenditure cuts. This is without allowing for any additional investment to aid in abating pollution and providing additional supplies of energy.[31]

Conclusions. The fiscal 1976 budget and subsequent changes by the Congress have apparently produced a "turnaround" in the long-run budget outlook from that indicated by the 1974 budget. The current outlook suggests that spending proposals and the 1975 tax cut will produce a sizable budget deficit, with an unemployment rate of 4.7 percent through 1977. We have apparently returned to the pre-1974 budget outlook, when it was widely estimated that the long-run impact of federal programs in effect would consume all, or virtually all, of the growth in full-employment revenues.[32] Without other spending cuts or tax increases it seems likely now that there will not be room for major new programs, such as sharply accelerated defense spending, implementation of national health insurance, or other social programs. The built-in growth in revenues between 1975 and 1978 will not make it possible to provide a balanced full-employment budget without having to cut back presently planned program initiatives or provide new sources of receipts. The battle for control of the budget is still very much in progress.

---

30 See Tilford Gaines, "Financial Implications of Material Shortages," *Economic Report* (Manufacturers Hanover Trust Company, November 1973); and Murray L. Weidenbaum, "The Government Competition for Investment Funds," Tax Foundation, *Tax Review*, vol. 34 (November 1973).

31 Barry Bosworth and James Duesenberry, "Resource Claims in the 1980s" (Brookings Institution, April 1974; processed).

32 Schultze et al., *Setting National Priorities*, Chapter 13.